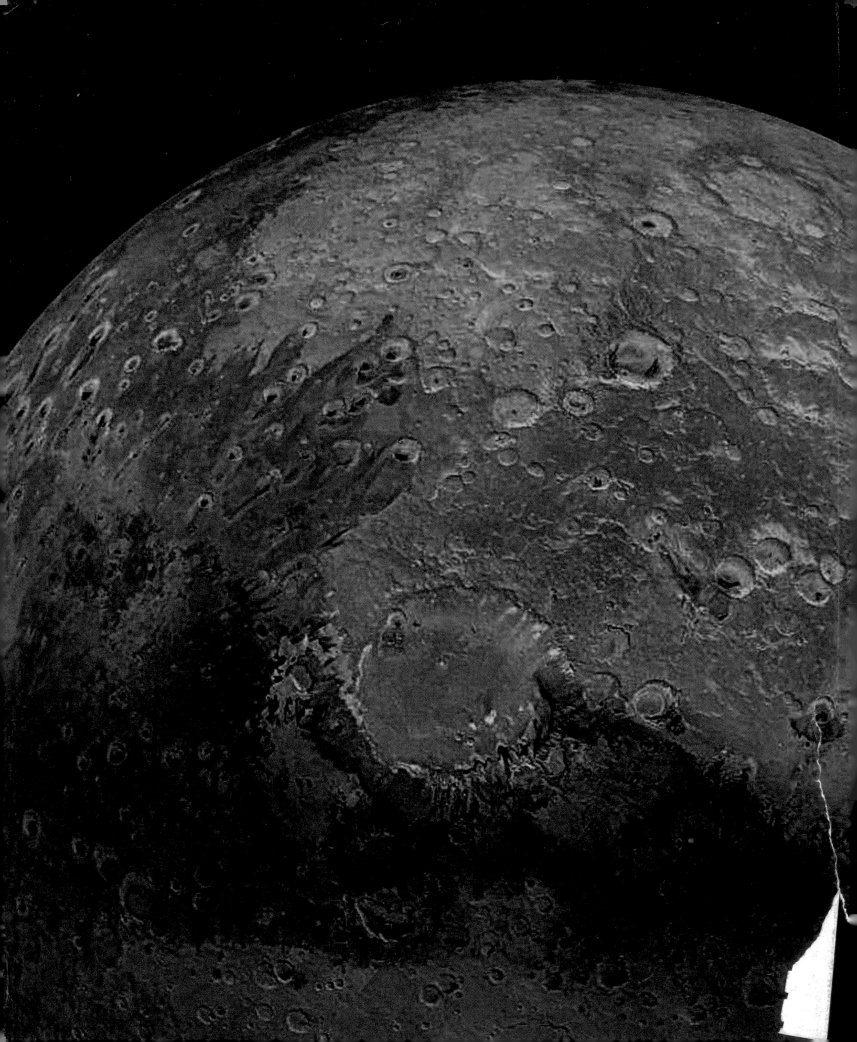

DISCOVER
MARS

BY GLORIA SKURZYNSKI

NATIONAL GEOGRAPHIC SOCIETY

WASHINGTON, D.C.

Published by the
National Geographic Society
1145 17th Street N.W.
Washington, D.C. 20036

John M. Fahey, Jr.,
*President and
Chief Executive Officer*

Gilbert M. Grosvenor,
Chairman of the Board

Nina D. Hoffman,
Senior Vice President

William R. Gray,
*Vice President and Director
of the Book Division*

Staff for this book:

Barbara Lalicki,
*Director of Children's
Publishing*

Marianne Koszorus,
Art Director

David M. Seager,
Designer

Suzanne Patrick Fonda,
Editor

Jennifer Emmett,
Assistant Editor

Mark A. Wentling,
Indexer

Vincent P. Ryan,
Manufacturing Manager

Lewis Bassford,
Production Manager

**The images for this book
were selected by Gloria
Skurzynski.**

**In this artist's rendition
(right) of the Pathfinder
mission, the rover Sojourner
sets out to explore Mars.**

**The end pages show, in 3-D,
one of the Twin Peaks. The
other peak appears on pages
28–29.**

**You will find the 3-D glasses
that come with this book
bound in after page 16.**

**Instructions for making
your own 3-D glasses are
on page 40.**

Library of Congress Cataloging-in-Publication Data
Skurzynski, Gloria.
    Discover Mars / by Gloria Skurzynski.
          p.   cm.
    Includes bibliographical references and index.
    Summary: Reviews results from the study of Mars, from
Copernicus through the Viking and Pathfinder missions, and
speculates on a future human landing.
      ISBN 0-7922-7099-1
    1. Mars (Planet)—Juvenile literature. [1. Mars (Planet)]
I. Title.
QB641.S496 1998
523.43—dc21

                     98-13190
                     CIP

Printed in the United States of America

The author is grateful to
Donna Shirley, the Mars program
manager, for so graciously sharing
information about Pathfinder
and Sojourner.

Along time ago, people thought that Earth was the center of the universe.

They saw the sun come up in the east and set in the west. At night, the moon, stars, and planets rose to creep across the sky, fading at daybreak. It seemed clear that all heavenly bodies moved around one center—the Earth.

Early in the 16th century, an astronomer named Nicolaus Copernicus studied the skies. Night after night, season after season, year after year, from a tower in what is now Frombork, Poland, Copernicus watched pinpoints of light move across darkness. He had no telescope, because telescopes hadn't yet been invented.

Copernicus watched the skies from this tower.

After many years of observation, Copernicus made a startling announcement. Earth is not the center of the universe, he said. Instead, "The sun rules the family of planets as they circle around it." Mercury, Venus, Mars, Jupiter, and Saturn all orbit the sun, Copernicus said. Because Earth rotates on its axis, we have days and nights.

Hardly anyone believed him.

But Copernicus was right.

Sixty-six years after Copernicus told of his discovery, a scientist named Galileo Galilei examined the heavens. Galileo had built himself a telescope, the first one ever used for studying the skies. His telescope was a wooden tube covered with red leather, decorated in gold, with lenses on both ends. It made stars and planets look 21 times larger than when seen with the naked eye.

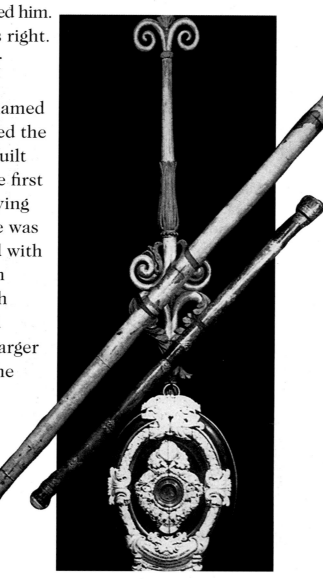

Galileo's first telescopes led to discoveries about our solar system, shown at right with orbits not to scale.

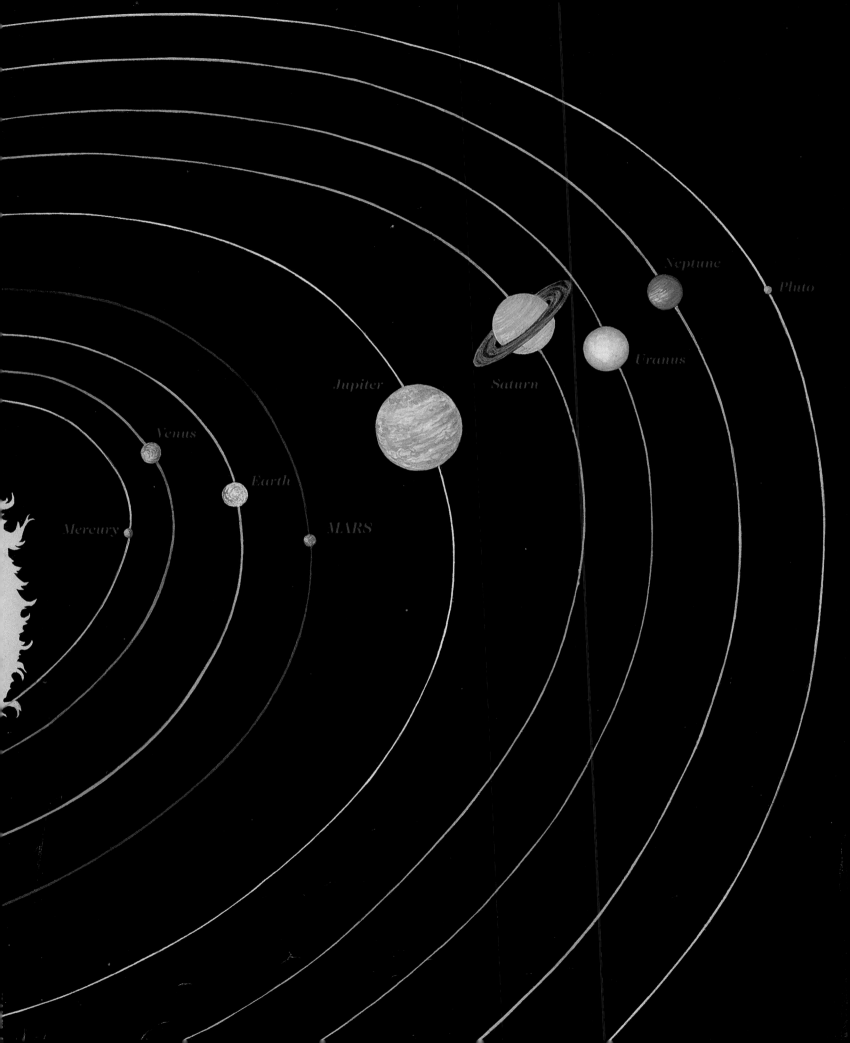

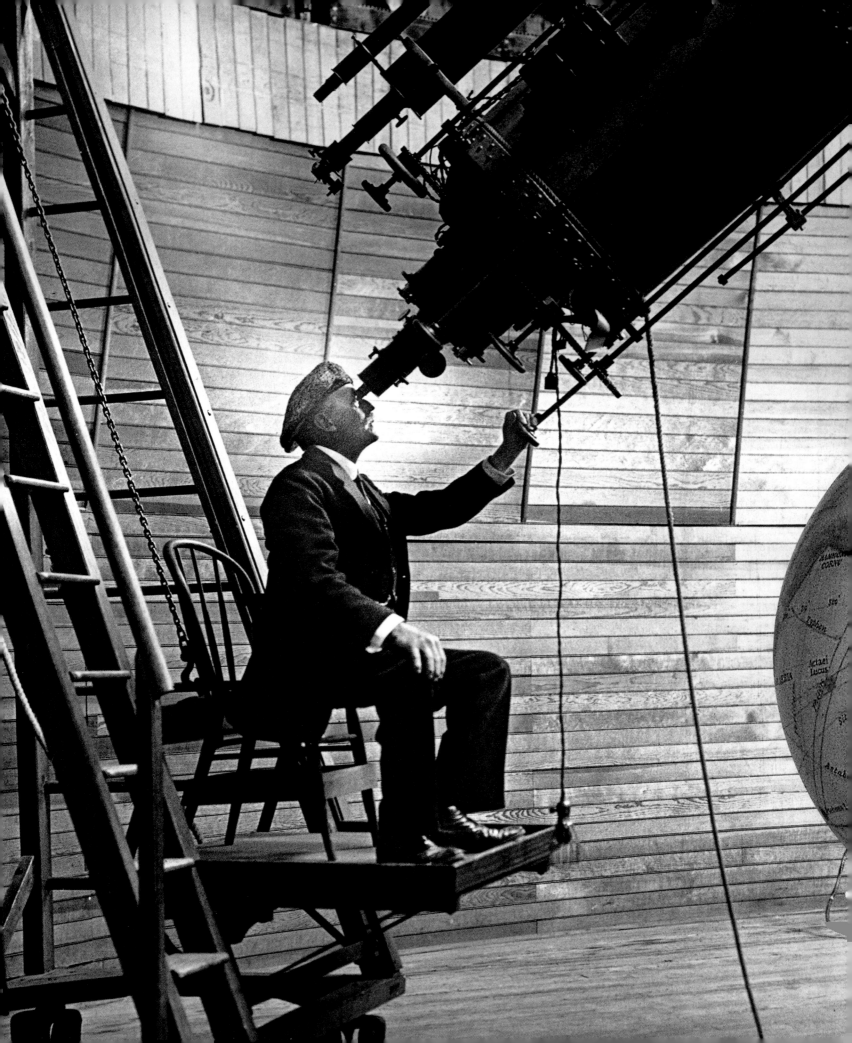

Over the next few hundred years, other astronomers built bigger and better telescopes. In Arizona in 1896, Dr. Percival Lowell installed a large telescope in an observatory named after him. He used it to search for intelligent life on the planet Mars.

With great excitement, Dr. Lowell announced that he had found canals on Mars. He believed they carried water from the polar ice caps, water that was being used to irrigate the dry, red, Martian soil.

These canals, he declared, must surely have been built by intelligent beings who lived on Mars. Peering through his telescope night after night, Dr. Lowell began to draw a map, on a globe, of the Martian canals.

Many people believed Dr. Lowell. But he was wrong.

Percival Lowell and his globe of Mars

*Mariner spacecraft
flew over Mars and
mapped the planet.*

There are no canals on Mars.

Why are we so sure of this? Because four spacecraft, looking like giant dragonflies and all named Mariner, have journeyed to Mars.

In 1965 Mariner 4 took 22 pictures from 6,000 miles above Mars and radioed them back to Earth. In 1969 Mariners 6 and 7 returned more pictures.

In November 1971 Mariner 9 began orbiting the red planet.

Over the next year its cameras took 7,300 photographs, covering 100 percent of the Martian surface. Not a single canal was seen.

All those images were taken from high above the planet. But in July 1976, the month of America's 200th birthday, Viking 1 landed on the surface of Mars.

As Viking 1 settled itself on the dusty red surface of Mars and sent its first signal to Earth, all the men on the project team—there were no women—jumped up to cheer wildly. Inside the Jet Propulsion Laboratory in Pasadena, California, the team members hugged and rejoice. Soft-landing a spacecraft, after a half-billion-mile, year-long journey, was a risky, hazardous job.

Viking 1 could have touched down on a big, jagged boulder and ripped the science instruments out of its underside. It could have sunk in powdery Martian dust or dropped into a deep crater. Any number of other things could have gone wrong.

Two months later, when Viking 2 landed safely on a different part of Mars, the scientists were both happy and relieved. Especially when the pair of landers started sending home pictures of their landing sites.

Touchdown! A Viking lander reaches Mars.

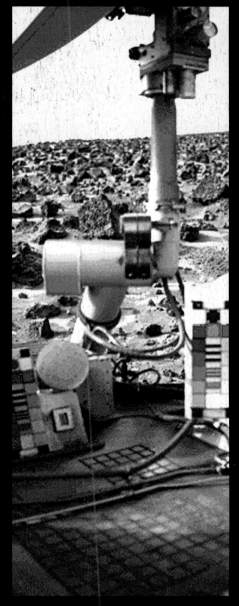

Viking 1 took pictures...

Both landers kept busy doing their assigned chores. With long-handled scoops, they dug up Martian soil and sucked it into each of three mini labs located in their insides. There the soil was sealed, irradiated, cooked, humidified, fed, measured, and analyzed. The results were radioed to Earth.

What were the scientists trying to discover? They were searching for signs of life. Percival Lowell, the man who mistakenly saw canals on Mars, said, "If astronomy teaches anything, it teaches that man is but a detail in the evolution of the universe. Though he will probably never find his double anywhere, he is destined to discover any number of cousins scattered through space."

The scientists were looking for some of those cousins. They hoped to find, perhaps, tiny bacteria in the red Martian soil. For months both of the Vikings' mini labs

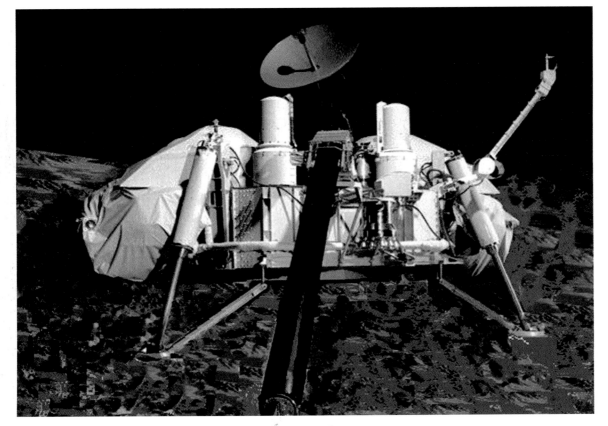

...and sampled the soil.

measured and analyzed and radioed data back to Earth. The results? Inconclusive. That means some of the scientists weren't quite sure about the results. Others were convinced that the Viking samples showed no signs of life.

And then, later, scientists found the first sign of possible Martian life. Not on Mars—on Earth!

One at a time, 12 Martian meteorites had been discovered on the ice of Antarctica. Scientists knew they'd come from Mars because gases trapped inside the rocks matched the gases Vikings 1 and 2 had measured in the Martian atmosphere.

Ten-year-old Ariel Boston is gazing at a piece of one of the 12 Martian meteorites. But a different one, with the unexciting name of ALH84001, was going to cause all kinds of excitement!

Ariel Boston, 10, studies a piece of Martian meteorite.

ALH84001: The bearer of ancient Martian life—maybe!

Shown here at its size when it was found, ALH84001 has had a fascinating history. It began 4.5 billion years ago, right after Mars was formed in our solar system. Not quite a billion years after that, the rock got cracked by a meteorite that hit Mars.

Fluid seeped into those cracks. Over the next 2 billion years or so, tiny globules of carbonate minerals formed in them. More meteorite strikes made more cracks. Then, 16 million years ago, one very powerful asteroid impact knocked ALH84001 out into space.

For almost that long the rock whirled around our solar system until, 13,000 years ago, it landed on Earth in Antarctica where, in 1984, a scientist found it.

Meteorites are always falling onto Earth. We don't notice them because most of them are small,

Meteorites are visible on snow.

and they look almost exactly like Earth rocks. On the frozen snow and ice of Antarctica, though, a dark meteorite is easy to spot.

Like the other known Martian meteorites, ALH84001 got sliced into sections for researchers to study (picture at top right). In laboratories all over the world, scientists measured and probed and analyzed the bits of rock.

Here are some of the things they reported:

•ALH84001 has certain molecules, mostly of carbon rings, that might have come from the decay of living things.

•A structure in those carbonates is similar to those on Earth that are formed by bacteria.

•Some mineral grains in the rock are similar to the ones produced by bacteria.

•And most impressive, some highly magnified images in the rock (bottom right) look a lot like fossils of bacteria found on Earth.

Notice the scientists say "might have" and "similar" and "look like." Never "for sure."

Scientists are always cautious about making statements. In this case they must be more careful than ever. Because to confirm that life exists, or once existed, on a place other than Earth would be, well—earthshaking! Even if the life consisted only of bacteria a hundred times smaller than any on Earth.

A thin slice of meteorite

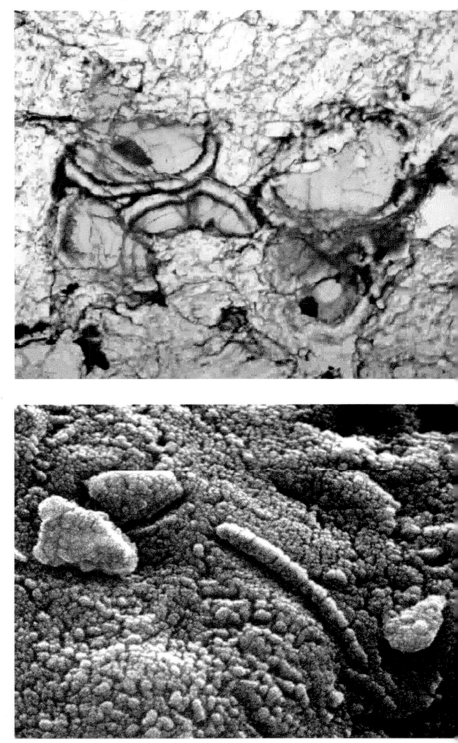

Ancient Martian microorganisms?

21

The scientists need more evidence. But it isn't easy to get. You can't just send up a space shuttle for some samples, because shuttles orbit at about 200 miles above Earth. When Mars is closest to Earth, it's still 35 million miles away.

Bringing Mars rocks back to Earth will be very hard to do, but not impossible. The Mariner flybys were the first step. The Viking landers and the spacecraft that have orbited Mars recently added valuable information on how to make this happen.

Another step, and the most exciting for many people, has been the Mars Pathfinder mission. On the Fourth of July, 1997, after a seven-month journey, Pathfinder landed on the red planet.

There had never before been a landing like this one. First a heat shield slowed the spacecraft from 18,000 miles per hour to 800 miles per hour. Six miles above Mars's surface, a parachute opened, slowing down the entry vehicle even more. Then, 294 feet above the surface, 17-foot-tall, segmented, balloonlike air bags inflated on each of the lander's four sides. The whole package looked like a giant raspberry.

At less than a hundred feet, the parachute was cut loose and the lander dropped. It bounced at least 15 times, rolled for a couple of minutes, then came to a stop—right side up! That was a bit of good luck.

Pathfinder had touched down on the flood delta of an ancient Martian valley named Ares. Geologists believe that, billions of years ago, the valley was carved by a flood equal to all the water in all five of our Great Lakes. Today, Ares is bone dry.

This artwork was made before the landing. Actually, Pathfinder landed at night, and the design of the air bags was slightly different.

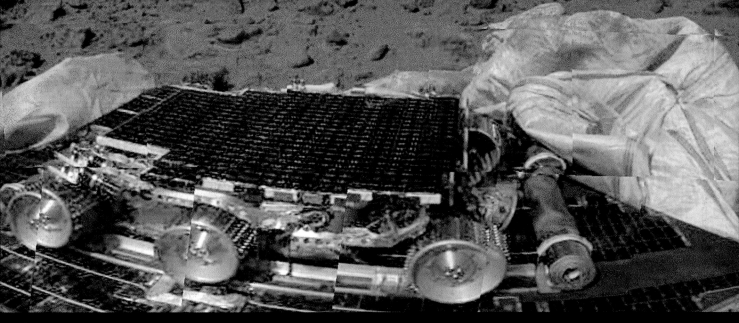

Safely landed

Pathfinder had landed safely. Once again the Mission Control room at Jet Propulsion Laboratory exploded with applause and cheers—and this time there were several women on the team.

Very soon Pathfinder's air bags were deflated and pulled back. Then three sides of the lander (it was sitting on the fourth side) opened like the petals of a flower. Inside, sat a 23-pound rover named Sojourner. After sunlight fell on its solar panels to provide power, Pathfinder's camera took a picture of the terrain, and of Sojourner.

Two ramps rolled out from the lander to the ground. For a while Sojourner just sat there on the petal of the lander, as if taking a look at this strange new place. Then she straightened herself up to her full 12-inch height and rolled down one of the ramps onto the Martian surface.

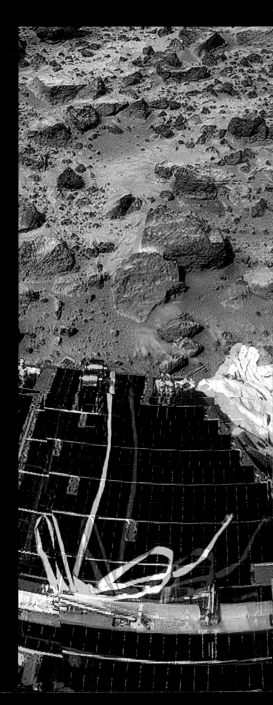

Back view of Sojourner

If the picture below looks strange, it's because it's meant to be viewed with red/blue glasses. These glasses—called anaglyph glasses—let you see things in 3-D! The red color must be in front of your left eye; the blue in front of your right eye. When you look through red/blue glasses, it may take you a few minutes to adjust to 3-D viewing. Experiment by holding the 3-D picture close to your eyes, then moving it farther away, an inch at a time. It helps to stare at one spot on the picture until the image comes together and the three dimensions "kick in."

Sojourner was ready to go to work.

Sojourner got in touch with a rock named Yogi.

One of Sojourner's main jobs was to "sniff" rocks. Her antenna and two cameras were on her front. Her round Alpha Proton X-ray Spectrometer—shortened to APXS—points out from the center of her back. You can see this clearly in the bottom picture on page 24.

The APXS can analyze the chemical makeup of Mars rocks and soil. Sojourner could back up to a rock, place her spectrometer close to its surface, and stay there for hours, analyzing. The rock named Yogi is basalt, the most common kind of rock in our solar system. The APXS found calcium, iron, silicon, and other minerals in Yogi.

Members of the Pathfinder team had fun naming the rocks they found on the Martian surface. Some were named for cartoon characters—Barnacle Bill, Scooby Doo, Ren, Stimpy, and Yogi. Others were given names that described their shapes—Couch, Chimp, Shark, Wedge, Flat Top, and Little Flat Top.

Sojourner had been named even before Pathfinder landed on Mars. "It was my rover," said Donna Shirley, the

Mars program manager. "I decided to name it after a woman. We never had a spacecraft named for a woman before."

A contest was held, worldwide. Students up to the age of 18 were invited to send in essays about their favorite heroines.

Valerie Ambroise of Connecticut entered an essay about Sojourner Truth, an African-American woman who lived during the time of the Civil War. Sojourner Truth made it her mission "to travel up and down the land, speaking out for the rights of all people," Valerie explained. "Sojourner" means "traveler."

Valerie, who was 12 at the time, wrote, "It's only logical that the Pathfinder be named Sojourner Truth, because she is on a journey to find truths about Mars."

The little rover named Sojourner traveled slowly across the Martian surface, avoiding rocks that might tip her over but moving close to the ones she would analyze.

Donna Shirley

Sojourner examined the Mini Matterhorn.

The Pathfinder lander, now named the Sagan Memorial Station after the late astronomer Carl Sagan, has sent 2.6 billion bits of information back to Earth. That includes 16,000 images from the lander and 550 from Sojourner. It will take years to study all these data, but scientists have already learned quite a lot.

This 3-D panorama of Mars terrain shows one of the Twin Peaks.

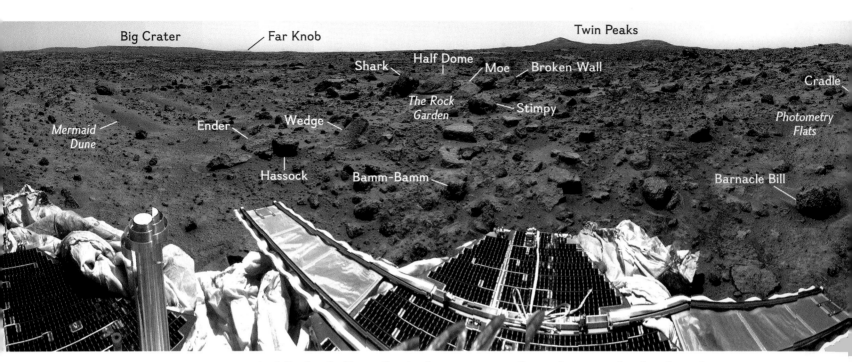

Big Crater   Far Knob   Twin Peaks

Shark   Half Dome   Moe   Broken Wall

Cradle

The Rock Garden   Stimpy

Photometry Flats

Mermaid Dune   Ender   Wedge

Hassock   Bamm-Bamm

Barnacle Bill

Wrinkled, deflated air bags stayed underneath the lander.

Water once flowed on the surface of Mars. Billions of years ago, a great flood swept across the Martian plain. The rocks Shark, Half Dome, and Moe are seen above, lined up pointing north, showing the direction the floodwaters must have flowed. In the distance, on the hills called Twin Peaks, there appear to be huge boulders left behind by the flood.

Since there once was liquid—unfrozen—water on Mars, the climate must have been warmer than today's average temperature of minus 100° F. Today on Mars, just inches above ground level, the temperature drops very quickly. If you stood on the planet's surface, your head would feel much colder than your feet.

Other discoveries: Mars has a core, but it is not a molten core like Earth's.

From Viking, scientists already knew about dust and rocks on Mars, but now for the first time they found pebbles and what could be sand. Iron minerals in the soil make the sand and dust red. Sunlight reflecting off blowing dust creates a pink sky.

Did the Pathfinder mission discover any forms of life on Mars? The answer is no.

But that doesn't mean life never existed on Mars.

Barnacle Bill was the first rock analyzed by Sojourner's APXS.

Said Henry Moore, one of the researchers with Sojourner, "Any Martians that ever lived may have been microscopic." The 15 rocks Sojourner analyzed were of a type different from ALH84001, the Martian meteorite. And Sojourner only examined the outsides of the rocks. She had no way to discover what might be inside them.

After 83 days on the surface of Mars, after 52 miles of back-and-forth trekking, Sojourner stopped sending data. All her messages had been radioed first to the lander, which then transmitted them to Earth. When the Martian summer ended and the frigid winter weather began, the lander's batteries wore out. It could no longer communicate.

But Sojourner kept trying to do her job. Each morning when the rising sun fueled her solar panels, the little rover would begin to circle the lander. She'd been programmed not to move too far beyond its reach. All day, like a lost kitten searching for her mother, Sojourner

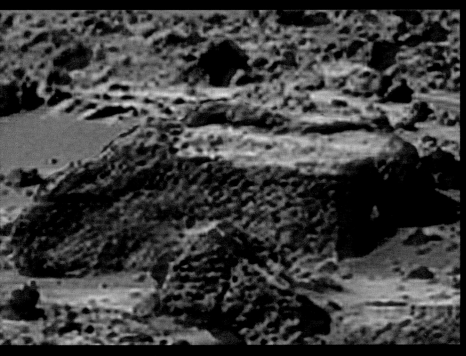

Iron minerals make the Martian surface red.

Sojourner examines Moe. Can you find it on page 30?

Mars Global Surveyor is studying the surface, atmosphere, and magnetic fields of Mars.

would wander around the landing site. She was waiting for the lander to wake up and tell her what to do.

As Pathfinder's lander stayed silent, a spacecraft orbited to within 75 miles above Mars. On its 10-month journey to reach the red planet, Mars Global Surveyor had traveled 466 million miles. It entered an elliptical orbit around the red planet and began to send us wide-angle pictures of Mars.

Once it reaches a circular orbit, the Global Surveyor will map every bit of the planet's surface for one whole Martian year (687 Earth days.) That will help us understand how Earth and Mars are alike, and how they're different.

Then, in March of 2001 and again in 2003, other orbiters will be launched to travel to Mars, followed by landers and rovers. More missions are scheduled to reach Mars every 26 months for a decade, each time Earth and Mars come closest to each other.

Although the 2001 rover will look like Sojourner, it will be bigger, and it will be able to travel farther. Designed to work for a whole year, it will carry a science payload called Athena.

Athena's main job will be to collect samples of Martian soil and rocks in places where evidence of life might be found.

Sojourner examined rocks, too, but only on the outside. Athena will have a tool called a mini corer that can drill into rocks—not just pebble-size or cobble-size rocks, but big boulders, and bedrock. She'll put the specimens into her sample container, a box with 91 storage bins for rock and 13 cups to hold loose soil.

Athena's mini corer

Then, in 2005, a different kind of spacecraft will arrive on Mars. All the other spacecraft were on one-way journeys—Earth to Mars. When their work was done, they stayed on the Martian surface, if they were landers and rovers. If they were orbiters, they relayed signals back to Earth until their equipment no longer functioned.

The 2005 mission will be the first to attempt a return trip. If all goes well, it will pick up Athena's sample box, carry it into the spacecraft, and blast off for Earth.

A Mars Sample Return Vehicle will bring Martian soils to Earth.

All these missions will prepare for the greatest adventure in history: the landing of humans on Mars. It might happen as early as 2011 if the massive preparations take place quickly and perfectly—funding, training, public support, the building of the Space Station, and the success of the next few missions of discovery are needed. With all that has to be done, though, it's more likely that humans won't reach Mars until closer to the year 2017.

Heading for Mars

Once they land on Mars, people can't be left behind like landers or rovers. They must be returned to Earth. This is how it might be done:

A Mars spacecraft will be launched to dock on the Space Station. After a second launch, this time from the Space Station—which will require less fuel because of low gravity— the spacecraft will begin its six-month journey to Mars.

Once on the Martian surface, the crew will use a rover to unload supplies.

Unloading supplies onto the Martian surface

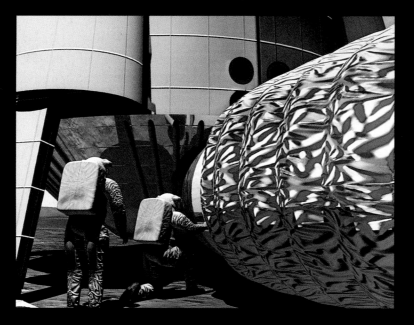

The laboratory, shown inflating (below), will be used to conduct experiments.

The inflated laboratory will connect to the two-story lander, where the crew will live.

People of many nations may be part of this
incredible journey. They'll search the surface for

It's easy to make your own 3-D glasses. You'll need red, blue, and black felt-tipped markers, scissors, and the clearest plastic you can find. Copy centers sell a heavy-gauge, clear-plastic sheet that's used for report covers. In the picture above, Zachary McCray is holding one of those cover sheets.

Place the clear-plastic sheet over the pattern below. With your red marker, outline the red area and color it on the plastic; do the same for the blue. Trace the outline of the glasses with a thin black marker. Allow at least 15 minutes for the colors to dry before you handle the glasses—otherwise they'll smear.

Then, with scissors, cut along the black outline. Hold the glasses in front of your eyes as Joshua Garcia is doing, red over your left eye, blue over your right.

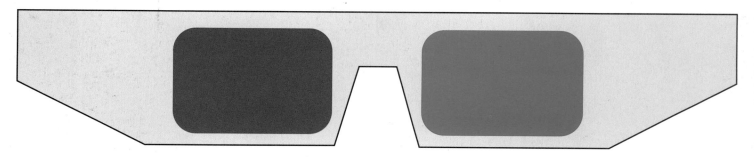

Use this pattern to trace your glasses.

This image was taken from 1,928 miles above Mars by the Viking 1 orbiter. View it in 3-D.

COOL WEB SITES ABOUT MARS

http://www.kyes-world.com/marsinter.htm
http://spacekids.hq.nasa.gov/mars/home.htm
http://mars.jpl.nasa.gov/mpf/anaglyph-arc.html
http://mars.jpl.nasa.gov/default.html
http://mars.jpl.nasa.gov/2001/timeline.html
http://photojournal.jpl.nasa.gov
http://quest.arc.nasa.gov/mars
http://mars.sgi.com/worlds/CyberMarz/Mars/HTML/index.html
http://alt.deol.ru/~queen/mars/03marsft.jpg
http://hyperion.advanced.org/13908
http://planetary.org/explorers-red-rover.html
http://humbabe.arc.nasa.gov/

http://mpfwww.jpl.nasa.gov/mpf/education/cutouts.html
(a site where you can find directions to build a Mars Pathfinder Spacecraft model!)

These sites are linked to other great sites.
Follow the links to learn everything about Mars and
the other planets in our solar system.

ORDERING 3-D ANAGLYPH GLASSES

You can order 3-D glasses from the following places:

Reel 3-D Enterprises
P.O. Box 2368
Culver City, California 90231

phone: 310-837-2368
fax: 310-558-1653
Web site:
http://www.stereoscopy.com/reel3d

Rainbow Symphony, Inc.
6860 Canby Avenue, Suite 120
Reseda, California 91335

phone: 818-705-8400
fax: 818-708-8470
Web site:
http://www.rainbowsymphony.
com/marsprice.html

American Paper Optics
2005 Nonconnah Blvd., Suite 27
Memphis, TN 38132

phone: 800-767-8427
or 901-398-6111
fax: 901-398-6119
Web site:
http://www.tisco.com/
3d-web/apo.htm

anaglyph – A combination of two almost identical, overlapping images, one red and one blue. Through red/blue glasses, a three-dimensional picture becomes visible.

antenna – A device for sending and receiving radio waves.

APXS – The Alpha Proton X-ray Spectrometer detects the chemical elements in a rock surface by analyzing the energy spectrum of its alpha particles.

astronomer – A scientist who studies heavenly bodies such as galaxies, stars, comets, planets and their satellites.

axis – A straight line, real or imagined, that a body rotates around.

carbonate – A chemical compound that forms in carbon dioxide and water.

delta – Land that forms from soil washed into the mouth of a river.

digital code – Information sent in bits: 1s and 0s.

galaxy – A grouping of cosmic dust, gas, and billions of stars held together by gravity. There are billions of galaxies in the universe.

geologist – A scientist who studies the formation of a planet's crust.

gravity – A force that pulls two bodies toward each other.

humidify – To make moist or damp.

irradiate – To bombard with x-rays or other forms of radiant energy such as ultraviolet waves.

lander – The part of a spacecraft that touches down on a planet's surface or on a moon.

magnetic field – An area where lines of magnetic force are detected. A magnetic field shields a planet from electrically charged particles from the sun.

meteor – A streak of light caused by a piece of matter from outer space (a meteoroid) striking a planet's atmosphere.

meteorite – A rock from outer space that falls onto a planet or a moon.

observatory – A building for watching heavenly bodies.

orbit – The path of a body traveling around another body.

orbiter – The part of a spacecraft that orbits a planet or a moon.

payload – The cargo of a spacecraft.

polar ice caps – Frozen water on Earth's North and South Pole regions. On Mars, the polar ice caps are mostly made of frozen carbon dioxide.

rotate – To turn around a center or an axis.

rover – A moving robot that explores the surface of a planet or a moon.

solar panels – Winglike panels covered with solar cells. They convert energy from the sun into electrical power for a spacecraft.

solar system – A star, the planets that orbit it, and the satellites of those planets.

spacecraft – A vehicle for exploration beyond Earth's atmosphere.

Space Station – An Earth-orbiting laboratory where an international crew will live and work. It can be used as a launching site for spacecraft.

INDEX

PHOTO & ILLUSTRATION CREDITS

Courtesy Jet Propulsion Laboratory/NASA/Caltech: end pages, title pages, dedication page (art by Pat Rawlings); pages 16, 17, 18, 23 (art by Pat Rawlings); 24, 25, 26 (top), 27, 28, 29, 30, 31, 32, 33, 34 (art by Michael Carroll).
Photos by Gloria Skurzynski: copyright page, pages 11, 27 (top), 40.

Page 10: art by Jean Leon Huens.
Page 12: courtesy IMSS, Florence.
Page 13: art by Carol Schwartz.
Page 14: (left) courtesy Lowell Observatory, (right) courtesy Smithsonian Institution.
Page 19: Lynn R. Johnson, The *Salt Lake Tribune.*
Page 21: (top) courtesy Dr. Allan

Tremain, Lunar and Planetary Institute.
Page 35: Cornell University and NASA.
Page 41: courtesy Dr. Paul Schenk, Lunar and Planetary Institute.
Courtesy Johnson Space Center/NASA: pages 20, 21 (bottom), 36–39 (for NASA by John Frassanito & Assocs.); 45 (art by Pat Rawlings).

This artist's rendering shows Mars:
a future world to explore.